Contents

What are elephants? 4

What is a herd of elephants like? 6

Where do elephants live? 10

What do elephants eat? 14

How do elephants care for their young? 17

How do elephants rest and relax? 20

How do elephants communicate? 22

Does a herd ever change? 24

Do elephants in a herd fight? 26

What dangers does a herd face? 27

Elephant facts 29

Glossary 30

Find out more 31

Index 32

Any words appearing in the text in bold, **like this**, are explained in the Glossary.

What are elephants?

Elephants are the largest animals in the whole world that live on land. With their massive body, long **muscular** trunk and big ears these huge **mammals** have an unmistakable appearance. Some elephants also have **tusks**, which are special, long front teeth. An elephant's skin is grey-brown and wrinkled with very little hair, except on its tail and trunk. **Male** elephants are called **bulls**. **Female** elephants are called **cows** and they are usually slightly smaller than the bulls.

What is a trunk?

A trunk is really a very long upper lip and nose. The end of a trunk has two nostrils (nose holes) and pointed parts that can grip, sometimes called head fingers. An elephant's trunk is strong enough to lift giant logs, but the head finger is flexible enough to turn on a tap or pick up a small coin!

An adult male African elephant's trunk can be 2 metres long. An elephant can be 4 metres tall and weigh about 6 tonnes – that's as much as 80 people!

Life in a Herd

Elephants

Heinemann
LIBRARY

Richard and Louise Spilsbury

www.heinemann.co.uk/library

To order:
☎ Phone 44 (0) 1865 888066
🗎 Send a fax to 44 (0) 1865 314091
💻 Visit the Heinemann Bookshop at www.heinemann.co.uk/library to browse our catalogue and order online.

First published in Great Britain by Heinemann Library, Halley Court, Jordan Hill, Oxford OX2 8EJ, part of Harcourt Education.
Heinemann is a registered trademark of Harcourt Education Ltd.

Editorial: Nicole Irving and Georga Godwin
Design: Ron Kamen and Celia Floyd
Picture Research: Rebecca Sodergren and Ginny Stroud-Lewis
Production: Viv Hichens

Originated by Dot Gradations Ltd
Printed in China by WKT Company Limited

ISBN 0 431 18267 1 (hardback)
08 07 06 05 04
10 9 8 7 6 5 4 3 2 1
ISBN 0 431 18274 4 (paperback)
09 08 07 06 05
10 9 8 7 6 5 4 3 2 1

British Library Cataloguing in Publication Data

Spilsbury, Richard and Spilsbury, Louise
Animal Groups: Elephants – Life in a Herd
599.6'7156
A full catalogue record for this book is available from the British Library.

Acknowledgements

The Publishers would like to thank the following for permission to reproduce photographs:

Corbis/RF p. 26; Digital Vision p. 14; Images of Africa Photobank/Carla Signorini Jones p. 15 (top); National Geographic/Michael Fay p. 22; Nature Picture Library/Lockwood & Dattari p. 5; NHPA/Andy Rouse p. 12 (bottom); NHPA/Daryl Balfour pp. 12 (top), 20, 25; NHPA/Gerrard Lacz p. 24; NHPA/Hellio & Van Ingen p. 11; NHPA/Kevin Schafer p. 7; NHPA/Martin Harvey pp. 4, 6, 10; NHPA/Nigel J. Dennis pp. 13, 16; NPL/Richard Du Toit p. 23; Oxford Scientific Films/Clive Bromhall p. 15 (bottom); Oxford Scientific Films/Lee Lyon p. 27; Oxford Scientific Films/Martin Colbeck pp. 9, 17, 18, 19, 21, 28.

Cover photograph of the elephant herd, reproduced with permission of Corbis/Peter Johnson.

The Publishers would like to thank Colin Fountain for his assistance in the preparation of this book.

Every effort has been made to contact copyright holders of any material reproduced in this book. Any omissions will be rectified in subsequent printings if notice is given to the Publishers.

Kinds of elephants

There are two **species** (kinds) of elephants – African elephants and Asian elephants. African elephants, as their name suggests, live in Africa. They have larger ears than Asian elephants and their ears are a similar shape to Africa. Asian elephants' ears are a similar shape to India and they have a flat forehead. African elephants have trunks with two head fingers, while Asians have one. Both male and female African elephants can have tusks, but only some male Asian elephants have them.

Elephant groups

Each elephant is an individual. They each look slightly different and have different personalities. Some elephants are quiet or shy, while others are more confident. Female elephants are **social** animals and spend most of their lives as part of a large group. Most male elephants live in small groups apart from the females. A group of elephants is called a herd.

This is an Asian elephant. Can you see the differences between this and the African elephant on page 4?

5

What is a herd of elephants like?

Elephants form groups of different sizes. They usually live in herds of between 6 and 12 elephants, but there can be up to 50 in a group. Herds sometimes split into smaller groups for a short time, but they usually join up again to form the main herd. A herd is basically a group of **female** elephants from the same family. The **dominant** member of an elephant herd is the **matriarch**.

Who is the matriarch?

The matriarch is the oldest and most respected female in the herd. She is also usually the largest of the elephants. The matriarch usually leads the rest of the herd to food, water and places to rest. She decides on how fast the herd will move together and how far they will travel each day. She also defends her herd from danger, such as **predators**.

The matriarch (centre) is usually the largest and strongest elephant in a herd.

Who else is in the herd?

The other members of the matriarch's herd include her adult daughters and sometimes her sisters. **Calves** in the herd may be the children of the matriarch, or of her daughters or sisters. Young **male** calves stay in their mother's herd until they are adults.

Do bulls form herds?

Bulls usually live alone or in small herds with other bulls for most of their adult lives. These male herds are called **bachelor herds**. The dominant bull in a bachelor group is always the biggest. Unlike female herds, bachelor herds are not family groups. They are usually groups of unrelated males.

When two elephants meet, the younger or less important elephant often puts the tip of its trunk into the other elephant's mouth. This is a kind of polite greeting, as when humans kiss or shake hands.

Showing who's who

As well as size, there are other ways of telling which is the dominant animal in a herd of male or female elephants. The dominant elephant always stands tall – it keeps its head higher than less important elephants. He or she also keeps their trunk hanging down. Elephants that are less important move their trunks from side to side, keep their ears flat and their head at a lower level than the dominant elephant's head.

Why do elephants live in a herd?

One of the reasons elephants live in herds is because they can help each other. For example, female herd members help each other take care of and protect their young. Elephants also seem to live together for the same reasons humans do, because they care about each other.

Do male and female herds join up?

Bull herds join up with female herds when they and the cows are ready to breed. After breeding time, the male and female herds part ways again. At times when there is lots of food and water to be found in one place, many herds of females and males gather to enjoy the feast. In some parts of Africa up to a thousand elephants have been seen in one place!

A baby elephant will stay close to an adult for safety when the herd is on the move.

Where do elephants live?

African elephants live mostly in central and eastern Africa. They live in groups scattered across different countries south of the Sahara Desert, including Ghana, Kenya, Tanzania and Uganda. Most African elephants live in either forest **habitats** or **savannah**.

Where do Asian elephants live?

Asian elephant herds live in south-east Asian countries such as India, Sri Lanka, Burma and Vietnam. Asian elephants mainly live in forests. They prefer shady habitats with lots of trees. They live in different kinds of forest but they always choose groups of trees near water. Some Asian elephants even live on the Andaman Islands, a small group of islands east of India. Some of these elephants have been known to swim up to 28 miles (45 kilometres) between the islands!

Many African elephants live in savannah habitats. Savannah is open stretches of dry dusty land mostly covered with grass, with patches of trees and **shrubs**.

Elephant paths

Elephant herds follow the same routes across land from one place to another for many years. They travel long distances to and from different areas in different seasons. They do this to make sure they get enough food and water all year round. The herds knock down trees and other plants in their way and create their own roads, often known as elephant paths.

How do elephants swim?

Many elephants are excellent swimmers. They paddle along using their strong legs with only the tops of their big heads showing above the water. They use their trunks like snorkels so they can breathe when their mouths are under water.

Elepants can swim at around 2 miles (3 kilometres) per hour and can swim for several hours without a rest.

Living in hot places

Elephant herds live mainly in hot dry habitats so there is a risk they could overheat. They do not sweat to cool themselves down as people do, but if they get too hot, they flap their ears. The air cools the blood inside their ears, which then travels back into the elephant's body, making that cooler too. Elephants also avoid the heat by bathing in water or mud, or by resting in the shade during the hottest part of the day.

Elephants use their trunks to spray themselves with dust or dirt to act as a sunscreen to protect their skin.

Herds of elephants often cool down by wallowing in mud if water is scarce.

In a dry African desert area like this one, the elephant herd may need to travel widely to find the food and water they need to survive.

What are home ranges?

Herds of elephants live in particular parts of their habitat called home ranges. A home range is the area that a herd moves around and stays within. A home range contains everything that a herd needs to live, such as enough food, water and shelter.

Home ranges are larger in drier, more open places because elephants have to travel further to find what they need. **Bachelor herds** live in separate ranges that do not usually overlap with the **female** ranges. Bachelor herds generally travel further and faster than female herds because they do not have **calves** with them to slow them down. **Males** also travel long distances to find females ready to **mate** with them.

13

What do elephants eat?

Elephants are **herbivores** – they eat grass and a wide range of different plants. They also eat leaves and twigs from bushes and trees, fruit, roots and bark. Favourite treats include figs, mangoes, ginger root or coffee berries. Elephants do not just eat any plants they find. The **matriarch** leads the herd to the most **nutritious** food she can find in big quantities.

If a matriarch finds a tree with ripe fruit the herd may stay at the tree for hours, until all of the fruit is gone.

How much do elephants eat?

A large adult elephant may eat up to 300 kilograms in a day – that's the weight of about 600 loaves! Elephants need to eat a lot because they are such large animals. Also, plant foods do not contain a lot of **nutrients** so herbivores have to eat a lot of plants to get all the nutrients they need. Elephants spend about 16 hours every day feeding!

How do elephants get their food?

Elephants use their trunks and **tusks** to gather and carry food. Elephants can use their long trunks to reach leaves at the top of trees, or to shake a tree to make fruit and nuts fall to the ground. They also bend trees over or snap branches off to get to the leaves at the top. Elephants use their tusks to scrape off bits of soil or soft rock. They eat these things because they contain important **minerals**, such as salt, which they cannot get from the plants they eat.

Elephants use their tusks to strip bark off trees. They eat bark in the **dry season** when there are fewer leaves and less fruit about.

These elephants are scraping bits of rock from the walls of a deep cave in Kenya.

How much water do elephants drink?

Elephants drink around 200 litres of water each day – that is about 14 buckets-full! In the dry season elephants do not travel around so much, because they need to stay near their water supply. Elephants have a pouch near their tongue that can store about 4 litres of water for emergency use.

An elephant's teeth

An elephant's tusks are special long sharp cutting teeth. They grow throughout its life. Elephants chew their food using just four flattish **molars** in the back of their mouths. When these teeth get worn down by grinding tough food, new ones push up from behind to replace them. An elephant has six sets of molars. These are all worn out by the age of about 60. At this age an elephant can die of starvation, because it can no longer chew its food.

An elephant drinks by sucking up water into its hose-like trunk and then blowing the water into its mouth.

Female elephants are old enough to have babies when they are between 9 and 15 years old. After **male** and female elephants **mate**, a baby takes nearly two years to develop inside the female before it is born. The male and female do not usually stay together after mating. The other elephants in the herd help to look after the mother and the **calf** when it is born.

An elephant's birth

All the elephants in the herd stay close by when a calf is born. They become very excited and make lots of rumbling noises. During birth, two or three other females stay with the mother. A mother elephant gives birth standing up. Elephant calves weigh between 75 and 110 kilograms, which is the weight range of an average adult man.

Adult females only give birth once every five years so when a new calf is born it is an important event for the whole herd.

17

What do calves look like?

An elephant calf is pinkish-grey and looks like a small version of an adult elephant but with a covering of coarse hair over its body. A calf stands up within half an hour of being born. Then it can reach its mother to **suckle** from teats between her front legs. Calves can follow their mother and the herd within a day or two.

Calves drink over 10 litres of milk a day for their first year. They suckle for about three years and then they start to eat plants. Calves suckle with their mouth, not their trunk.

Do elephants make good mothers?

A mother elephant is very protective and stays close by her calf until it is about five years old. She tucks it between her legs to hide it from **predators** or strong sun. She washes and cools it by squirting water over it and lets it try new foods by taking them from her mouth.

Calves and the herd

The whole herd helps to look after the calf. A calf can suckle from other females in the herd as well as its mother. If the herd meets a predator or an elephant that the group does not know that might harm the calf, it forms a circle around the calf to protect it. Calves learn about what to eat, where to find water and how to behave by watching the other herd members. Calves also watch others to learn their place in the herd and to show respect to the **matriarch**.

Babysitters

Young female elephants in the herd often act as baby-sitters. This gives them a chance to learn how to care for babies. This is important so that they will make good mothers when they have calves of their own.

A mother elephant uses her trunk to slap the calf when it is naughty, cuddle or stroke it to calm it, and to steer it along!

How do elephants rest and relax?

Elephants relax and cool down by bathing in water or mud every day, if they have the chance. After bathing, they often shower dust over their bodies with their trunk. Then they rub their body against something, like a tree trunk. Doing this helps to get rid of the tiny insects that live in the folds of their thick skin and irritate them.

Calves rest out of the sun during the hottest hours of the day, often beneath their mother's legs. Adults rest too if they can find a shady spot.

When do elephants sleep?

Elephants only sleep for about five hours a night. Younger elephants mainly sleep lying down on one side. Older elephants usually sleep standing up because it is difficult for them to get up after lying down. They may lean against something, such as a tree, to make themselves more comfortable.

Do elephants play?

Calves play alone or together in groups. They splash about in water, push and butt each other, trunk–wrestle and roll over. Mums or young adult females may stop fights if they get too rough and if little ones are knocked over. Adults and calves may play by picking up and throwing plants and even small trees about, spraying water from their trunks and chasing each other about.

A close-knit herd

Elephants stay near to each other when they rest and relax as well as when they feed. They show affection by touching each other often. While they are resting they often lean or rub against each other. Mothers cuddle their calves with their trunk.

Elephant calves are very playful. Games like these are fun but they also help elephants get to know others in the herd. They also develop strength and fighting skills that will be useful later in life.

How do elephants communicate?

Elephants cannot see very well so they **communicate**, or tell each other things, mainly using their other senses – sound, touch and smell.

What sounds do elephants make?

An elephant's large ears help to funnel sound so they have excellent hearing. Elephants make many different sounds, each with different meanings. For example, they make deep rumbling sounds that can travel over long distances to keep in touch with each other. They may make a sort of growling sound to call to the **matriarch** if they get lost. They roar to threaten **predators** or people. If a **calf** squeals for help or moans to complain the whole herd might go over to comfort it!

This elephant is making a trumpet sound by straightening its trunk and blowing air through its nostrils. Trumpeting can be an alarm call, an angry call or a cry for help.

How do they communicate by touch?

Elephants often communicate by touch. For example, they may touch trunks to greet each other or shake trunks with a stranger to find out who they are and if they are friendly. **Males** and **females** twine their trunks together when they are deciding whether to **mate**. Calves put their trunks into their mother's mouth to feel comforted.

Communicating by smell

Elephants have a very good sense of smell. They use their trunk to sniff dung, urine (wee) or scents that other elephants have rubbed on to things such as trees. Elephants in a herd can tell whether the smells were made by unrelated elephants or related ones. Elephants also sniff each other when they meet. They do this so they get to know other elephants well and learn to recognize other individuals.

An elephant's trunk is covered in small hairs. These make the trunk very sensitive so it can feel the slightest touch from another elephant.

Does a herd ever change?

Herds of elephants change over time. **Females** usually stay with the herd for their whole lives. As **males** get older they spend more time away from the herd. At around twelve years old they leave their mother's herd for good and join a **bachelor herd**.

Bachelor herds often change. From about the age of fifteen years old each **bull** has a short time each year when he is ready to **mate**. During these times he becomes aggressive and excitable and he leaves the bachelor herd. He seeks out a herd of females and stays with them until one or several of them are ready to mate with him.

As female **calves** get older, they start to show more interest in looking after the youngsters in the herd.

What happens if a matriarch dies?

A **matriarch** will carry on leading her herd until she dies. When she dies, her eldest daughter usually becomes the **dominant** elephant in the herd. If a matriarch dies suddenly, if for instance hunters shoot her, the herd often panics. Rather than leave her, the other elephants may stay by the matriarch, even though they may be shot themselves. Sometimes the herd splits up because of a matriarch's sudden death.

Old male elephants often cannot keep up with the young bulls in a bachelor herd. They stay alone in places where they can find food easily, such as swamps where there are soft plants they can chew easily with their worn-down teeth.

Death ceremony

When an elephant dies the other members of the herd gather round the body. Sometimes they cover the body with twigs and dirt. They stay near the body for hours and seem to show great sadness at their loss.

Do elephants in a herd fight?

Elephants in a herd do squabble and tussle, but they rarely fight. Most arguments happen at **breeding** time, between **bulls** wanting to **mate** with the same **female**, but bulls also fight over food or water. Most disagreements are sorted out using **displays**. For example, an elephant may spread its ears to make itself look bigger. Or it might curl and uncurl its trunk and shake its head. Usually this is enough for one elephant to prove to another that it would win if they fought, so the other elephant allows itself to be chased off.

If displays don't work, the two bulls still do not fight. They check each other's strength by pushing down on each other's trunk from above and grappling with their trunks. If one still does not give in, they may fight. Fights can be ferocious – elephants charge, grapple and push to try to stab each other in the side with their **tusks**.

Elephants size each other up before a fight. This allows the weaker of the two to back off and avoid being injured in a real battle.

What dangers does a herd face?

Adult elephants have few **predators** because of their size and strength. Lions, tigers, crocodiles or hyenas can kill young or very old and weak elephants. If a predator approaches, the herd usually manages to protect **calves** by forming a circle around them. The greatest threat to an elephant herd is people.

People and elephants

One of the main reasons that people kill elephants is to take their **tusks**. Tusks are made of ivory, which people once made piano keys from and still use for decorative objects like carvings. There are laws to protect elephants, but ivory is very valuable so **poachers** are prepared to risk getting caught. Poachers try to catch the elephants with the biggest tusks in a herd, which usually means the **matriarchs**. Poaching is less of a problem for Asian elephants because fewer Asian elephants have tusks.

The matriarch and other herd members will charge towards an enemy to try to chase it away.

Elephant habitats

People also affect elephants when they cut down forests to use the wood or clear land for farming and building. When this happens, people take over land that elephants used to live in or travel across to find food or other elephants to **mate** with. People may kill elephants if they eat or trample their crops (food plants).

Park rangers patrol national parks in jeeps or on foot to stop poachers from harming the elephants that live there.

Who helps elephants?

As a result of poaching and **habitat** loss, African and Asian elephants are now **endangered species**. This means they might one day become extinct (die out). Some **conservation** groups, such as WWF, are working to protect elephants and to educate people about the importance of saving elephants. There are also **national parks** in Africa and India where elephants and other animals should be able to live safely.

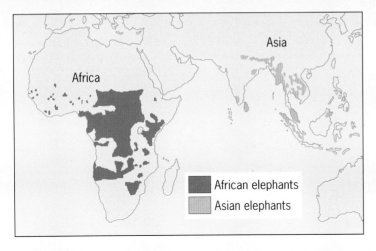

This map shows where wild African and Asian elephants live. There are between 300,000 and 600,000 African elephants altogether, living in 37 different countries. There are 35,000 to 50,000 Asian elephants, living in 14 different countries.

Is it true that elephants never forget?

Elephants are very intelligent and they do have remarkable memories. Elephant herds rely on the memories of their **matriarchs**. She remembers where the best food sources are and when a herd meets another elephant she remembers whether it is a friend or enemy.

Are elephants scared of mice?

Elephants are not frightened of mice or rats. This story probably came about because sudden, unexpected noises or movements do scare them. If a mouse or rat scurried past suddenly, this could easily startle an elephant.

Lifespan

Elephants can go on having young every few years until they are about 50 years old. They can live until they are 60 or 70 years old.

Beasts of burden

For many years people have used Asian elephants to carry people, logs and other heavy objects. African elephants are hardly ever used in this way, although some are trained for circus shows.

Glossary

bachelor herd   herd of male elephants

breed/breeding   have babies

bulls   male elephants

calves   baby elephants

communicate   pass on information to another animal

conservation   action to stop wild animals, plants and places from dying out or being destroyed

cows   female elephants

display   put on a show of actions or movements that sends a message to another animal

dominant   leader of a group or most important member

dry season   months when it may not rain at all

endangered species   plant or animal in danger of becoming extinct (dying out)

female   animal that, when mature, can become a mother. A female human is called a girl or woman.

habitat   place where an animal or plant lives

herbivores   animals that eat only or mainly plants and plant parts

male   animal that, when mature, can become a father. A male human is called a boy or a man.

mammal   group of animals that includes humans. All mammals feed their babies milk from their own bodies and have some hair.

mate   after a male and female animal have mated, a baby begins to grow inside the female

matriarch   leader of the herd and the oldest female in the herd

mineral   chemical found in rocks and soil. Animals need several different minerals to be healthy.

molars   flat-topped teeth at the back of an animal's mouth

muscular   full of muscles. Muscles are parts of the body that help to make the bones and the rest of the body move.

national park   area of natural beauty that is protected by law so that people cannot change or damage it or the plants and animals that live in it

nutrients   kinds of chemicals found in food that animals need to be healthy

nutritious   when food contains nutrients

poachers   people who hunt and kill wild animals illegally

predators   animals that hunt or catch other animals to eat

savannah   areas of dusty ground covered in grasses, patches of trees and shrubs

shrubs   plants with woody stems like trees that do not grow taller than about 6 metres

social   living in a group

species   group of living things that are similar in many ways and can reproduce together

suckle   when a baby mammal drinks milk from its mother's body

tusks   special, long front teeth of an elephant

Find out more

Books

Animal Family: The Elephant Family Book, Oria Douglas-Hamilton and Iain Douglas-Hamilton (North-South Books, 1996)

Eyewitness Guides: Elephant, Ian Redmond (Dorling Kindersley, 2000)

In the Wild: Elephants, Patricia Kendell (Hodder Children's Books, 2002)

Oxford Reds: Elephants, Paul May (Oxford University Press, 2001)

Websites

www.nationalgeographic.com has a children's section with creature features. The African elephant section has facts, information and video and audio features.

www.panda.org is the website of WWF. The site has lots of information about African and Asian elephants and suggestions for how you can help to protect them.

www.bbc.co.uk/nature has several articles about elephants and information in the wildfacts and really wild sections.

www.pbs.org/wnet/nature/elephants has lots of information, pictures and links about African elephants.

Index

African elephants   4, 5, 10, 28, 29
Asian elephants   5, 10, 27, 28, 29

bachelor herds   5, 7, 9, 13, 24, 25

calves   7, 13, 17–19, 20, 21, 22, 23, 24, 27
communication   7, 21, 22–3
conservation   28
cool, keeping   12, 18, 20

dangers   6, 18, 19, 22, 25, 27, 27–8
death   16, 25
displays   26
dominant elephants   6, 7, 8, 25

ears   4, 5, 22, 26
elephant paths   11
endangered species   28

female elephants (cows)   4, 5, 6, 7, 13, 14, 17, 19, 21, 22, 23, 24, 25, 27, 29
fights   26
food and water   11, 13, 14–16, 18, 25, 29

habitat loss   28
habitats   10, 12, 29
herbivores   14
herds   5, 6, 7, 8, 9, 11, 12, 13, 24, 25, 26
home ranges   13

ivory   27

lifespan   29

male elephants (bulls)   4, 5, 7, 8, 13, 23, 24, 25, 26
mammals   4
mate   13, 17, 23, 24, 26
matriarchs   6, 14, 19, 22, 25, 27, 29
memories   29

national parks   28

play   21
poachers   27, 28
predators   6, 18, 19, 22, 27

rest periods   20, 21

savannah   10
size and weight   4, 17
skin   4, 20
sleeping   20
smell, sense of   23
sounds   17, 22
suckling   18, 19
swimming   10, 11

teeth   16
trumpeting   22
trunks   4, 5, 7, 12, 15, 16, 19, 21, 23, 26
tusks   4, 5, 15, 16, 26, 27

working elephants   29